C901599998

THE FUNNIEST HOLIDAY JOKE BOOK EVER

2 2 DEC 2017

D1589715

THE FUNNIEST HOLIDAY JOKE BOOK EVER

By Joe King

Illustrated by Nigel Baines

Andersen Press

This edition first published
in Great Britain in 2014 by
Andersen Press
20 Vauxhall Bridge Road
London SW1V 2SA
www.andersenpress.co.uk

Text copyright © Andersen Press, 2014
Illustrations copyright © Nigel Baines, 2014

All rights reserved. No part of this publication may be
reproduced, stored in a retrieval system or transmitted
in any form, or by any means, electronic, mechanical,
photocopying, recording or otherwise, without the
written permission of the publisher.

The moral right of the illustrator has been asserted.

British Library Cataloguing in
Publication Data available.

ISBN 978 1 78344 109 9

Printed and bound in Great Britain by
CPI Group (UK) Ltd,
Croydon, CRO 4YY

Bonkers Holidays

Why do elephants have trunks?
*Because they would look
funny with a suitcase*

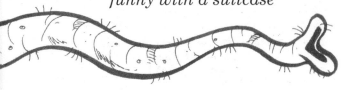

What is grey, has four legs, a tail, and a trunk?
A mouse on holiday

Why did the pirate go on holiday?
For some arrrrrgh and arrrrrgh

**Where do genies go
on summer holiday?**
To lamp camp

**What stays in the corner, but
travels round the world?**
A stamp

**What's the best thing to
give a seasick elephant?**
Plenty of room

**Where do werewolves stay
when they're abroad?**
At the Howliday Inn

**Why did Mickey Mouse
take a trip into space?**
He wanted to find Pluto

Going Places

How do fleas travel from place to place?
By itch-hiking

What part of the car is the laziest?
The wheels, because they are always tyre-d

What snakes are found on cars?
Windshield vipers

Who drives away all his customers?
A taxi driver

Which bus crossed the Atlantic?
Columbus

How do fish get around the seabed?
They go by octobus

**Why did the bat
miss the coach?**
*Because he hung around
for too long*

**What did the bus conductor
say to the frog?**
'Hop on!'

**What's green, has four legs
and two trunks?**
Two seasick tourists

**Did you hear about the boat
carrying red paint that
crashed into a boat
carrying blue paint?**
The crew was marooned

What's the worst vegetable to serve on a boat?
Leeks

Why did the sailboat sink while tied to the dock?
Pier pressure

Where does a ship go when it's sick?
To the dock-tor

There was terrible weather on the ferry crossing.

STEWARD: Would you care for some more supper, madam?

PASSENGER: *No, thanks. Just throw it overboard to save me the trouble!*

What do you give a train driver for her birthday?
Platform shoes

How do trains hear?
Through their engine-ears

How do you find a missing train?
Follow its tracks

Why was the railroad angry?
Because people were always crossing it

What's the difference between a train and a teacher?
The teacher says, 'Spit your gum out!' and the train says, 'Choo-choo!'

SON: When I grow up I want to drive a train.

DAD: *Well, I won't stand in your way.*

Hit The Road

What is the difference between a flashing red traffic light and a flashing yellow traffic light?
The colour

**When driving through fog,
what should you use?**
Your car

**A policeman saw a man
knitting and driving
at the same time and
shouted, 'Pull over!'**
*'No,' the man shouted back,
'a scarf!'*

**What do you do when
you see a spaceman?**
Park your car in it, man

**When is a car driver
not a car driver?**
When she turns into a side road

**Why did the dog
cross the road?**
To get to the barking lot

**Why did the duck
cross the road?**
To prove he wasn't chicken

**Why did the cow
cross the road?**
To get to the udder side

**Why did the dinosaur
cross the road?**
*Because chickens hadn't
evolved yet*

A policeman pulls over a busload of tourists.

POLICEMAN: Sir, the speed limit on this motorway is seventy – why are you going so slow?

DRIVER: *Sorry officer, I saw lots of signs that said twenty, not seventy.*

POLICEMAN: Sir, that's not the speed limit, that's the name of the motorway you're on!

DRIVER: *Silly me! Thanks for letting me know.*

The policeman notices all the passengers are shaking and trembling.

POLICEMAN: What's wrong with your friends back there?

DRIVER: *Oh, we just got off the M180!*

High Flyers

CALLER: How long does it take to get to New York?

TRAVEL AGENT: *Just a minute. . .*

CALLER: Wow, faster than I thought!

A man was driving to the
airport. He saw a sign
that said 'Airport: left.'
So he went home.

GIRL: I hope this plane doesn't
travel faster than sound.

FLIGHT ATTENDANT: *Why?*

GIRL: Because my friend
and I want to talk!

BOY: Do you have any helicopter-flavoured crisps?

FLIGHT ATTENDANT: *No, we only have plane.*

Did you hear about the pilot who always had work?
He was great at landing a job

What did the pilot do when she discovered her son had been naughty?
She grounded him

Have you heard the joke about the plane?
No? Well, it was way over your head anyway

During her flying test a young
pilot flew through a rainbow.
She passed with flying colours.

What do you call an ejector seat
on a helicopter?
A bad idea

Why did the girl wear a
watch on the plane?
She wanted to see time fly

What do you get if you cross a
dog and a plane?
A jet setter

Why did the girl study
on the plane?
She wanted a higher education

**What kind of plates do
they use on planes?**
Flying saucers

**What do you call a
flying policeman?**
A heli-copper

**What's red and flies and
wobbles at the same time?**
A jelly-copter

**What did the fly say when
it smacked into the plane's
windscreen?**
*'I don't have the guts
to do that again!'*

**What airline do
vampires travel on?**
British Scareways

What's big, hairy and can fly?
King Koncorde

**Did you hear about the pig
that took a plane?**
The swine flew

Where do rabbits learn to fly?
The Royal Hare Force

**What is black and yellow and
buzzes along at 30,000 feet?**
A bee in a plane

Life's a Beach

What do you call a witch who lives by the seaside?
A sand-witch

What do you call a man with a seagull on his head?
Cliff

What do you call a girl who's good at catching fish?
Annette

**Why do seagulls fly
over the sea?**
*Because if they flew over the bay
they would be bagels*

**Where do you learn to
make ice cream?**
Sundae school

**Why did the boy hide after he
stole a beach inflatable?**
He had to lilo for a while

**What did the sea say
to the sand?**
Nothing, it just waved

Lucy buys an ice cream at the seaside.

ICE-CREAM MAN: Would you like hundreds and thousands?

LUCY: *No, just one, please!*

What is hairy and coughs?
A coconut with a cold

Why can't you starve to death on a beach?
Because of the sand which is there

What washes up on very small beaches?
Microwaves

**What's the best day
to go to the beach?**
Sunday

**The seaside resort we went to
last year was so boring that
one day the tide went out and
never came back.**

**At the seaside Mum
was gazing at the
beautiful sunset.**

'Doesn't the sun look wonderful
setting on the horizon?' she said.

'Yes,' said her son, 'but won't it
fizz when it touches the water?'

Two lions are walking along the beach. One turns to the other and says, 'It's awfully quiet today isn't it?'

What did the sea say to the sand?
'I mist you!'

All at Sea

**What does a shark eat
for dinner?**
Fish and ships

**What kind of hair
do oceans have?**
Wavy

**What is the strongest
creature in the sea?**
A mussel

Why did the crab blush?
Because the seaweed

**Where do fish go to
the movies?**
At the dive-in

**Who is the biggest gangster
in the sea?**
Al Caprawn

**What do you get when you
cross a snowman and a shark?**
Frostbite

**How do you communicate
with a fish?**
Drop him a line

**What's the most musical
part of a fish?**
The scales

Why are some fish at the bottom of the ocean?
Because they dropped out of school

What's the difference between a guitar and a fish?
You can't tuna fish

What do you get when you cross fish and an elephant?
Swimming trunks

Why is it so easy to weigh fish?
Because they come with their own scales

**What is a fish's favourite
time of the day?**
Water to three

**What happens when you
throw a rock in the sea?**
It gets wet

**Which fish is the
most famous?**
The star fish

**How do oysters call
their friends?**
On shell phones

Where do fish sleep?
On a seabed

**Why did the whale
cross the ocean?**
To get to the other tide

**What is full of holes
but can still hold water?**
A sea sponge

**Where can you find an
ocean with no water?**
On a map

**What do you get when you
throw a million books
into the ocean?**
A title wave

**What lies at the bottom of the
ocean and twitches?**
A nervous wreck

Why did the shellfish go to the gym?
To get stronger mussels

Why didn't the shrimp have any friends?
Because he was a bit shellfish

**What do whales like to
eat at parties?**
Jellyfish

What's yellow and dangerous?
Shark-infested custard

Where do ghosts like to swim?
The Dead Sea

**Why doesn't the sea spill
over the earth?**
Because it's tide

**What do you use to cut the
ocean in half?**
A sea-saw

35

**How did the mussel
trim his beard?**
With a razor clam

**What's that gooey stuff in
between a shark's teeth?**
Slow swimmers

What is green and fluffy?
A seasick poodle

**Why do fish swim in
salt water?**
*Because pepper makes
them sneeze*

**Where does a fish go to
borrow money?**
A loan shark

**What is a shark's
favourite game?**
Swallow the leader

Pool Party

**What gets wetter the
more it dries?**
A towel

**Why shouldn't you swim
on a full stomach?**
*Because it's easier to swim in a
full swimming pool*

At the swimming pool, a man was on the very top diving board. He lifted his arms, preparing to jump off, when the lifeguard ran over shouting, 'Don't dive! There's no water in that pool!'

'That's all right,' said the man. 'I can't swim!'

What do swimmers eat off?
A pool table

Why did the teacher jump into the swimming pool?
She wanted to test the water

What kind of swimming stroke can you put on toast?
The butter-fly

Why can elephants swim whenever they want?
They always have trunks with them

In which direction does a chicken swim?
Cluck-wise

Camping Capers

**What did one campfire
say to the other?**
'Shall we go out tonight?'

Knock, knock
Who's there?
Wendy
Wendy who?
**Wendy you want
to go camping?**

BOY: Did you enjoy camping?

GIRL: *Not really, it got a little
too in-tents!*

BOY: Hey, look over there.
What's that?

GIRL: *Wow, smoke signals!*

BOY: What do they say?

GIRL: *Help . . . my . . .
blanket's . . . on . . . fire!*

Where did the dog sleep when it went camping?
In a pup tent

BOY: This is a good place for a picnic.

GIRL: *How do you know?*

BOY: All these flies and ants must know what they're doing!

Where do fish stay on a campsite?
In tentacles

Be Our Guest

What did one elevator say to the other elevator?
'I think I'm coming down with something!'

What do witches ask for at hotels?
Broom service

What did the blanket say to the bed?
'Don't worry, I've got you covered.'

Why should you take a pencil to bed?
To draw the curtains

Who should you call if there's a ghost in your hotel?
A hotel inn-spectre

SON: I can't get to sleep!

DAD: Lie on the edge of the bed and you'll soon drop off.

What has one head, one foot and four legs?
A bed

In a hotel in France, a man ordered his room service breakfast.

RECEPTIONIST: How many eggs would you like in your omelette?

MAN: *I think one egg is un oeuf.*

BOY: Why are you taking the stairs to the top floor?

RECEPTIONIST: *I usually take steps to avoid elevators.*

Why did the girl run around her bed?
She wanted to catch up on her sleep

WAITER: I'm looking for a job in the hotel restaurant.

HOTEL MANAGER: *Are you inn-experienced?*

A hotel receptionist received a call from one of the guests.

GUEST: Help! I'm trapped in my room!

RECEPTIONIST: *What do you mean?*

GUEST: I can only see three doors. The first one is to the bathroom, the next one opens the wardrobe, and the third door has a *Do Not Disturb* sign on it!

GUEST: Room service? I can't find a single towel in my room!

RECEPTIONIST: *Please wait, someone else is using it.*

GUEST: My room is swimming in water. Does the roof always leak like that?

RECEPTIONIST: *No, madam. Only when it's raining.*

GUEST: Why did you give me a fruit pastille?

RECEPTIONIST: *You said you wanted the best suite in the hotel.*

The hotel was filthy.
They changed the sheets
every day, but only
from one room to another.

What's For Dinner?

PATIENT: Doctor, I think I need glasses!

WAITER: *You certainly do, this is a restaurant!*

**What did the angry customer
at the Italian restaurant
give the chef?**
A pizza his mind

**Did you like the restaurant
on the moon?**
No, it had no atmosphere

**What did the fork
say to the knife?**
'You're looking sharp!'

**Where do burgers
like to dance?**
At a meatball

CUSTOMER: This food tastes
kind of funny.

WAITER: *Then why aren't
you laughing?*

**Why did the clock in the hotel
buffet run slow?**
It always went back four seconds

What did the duck say to the waiter when he couldn't pay for his dinner?
Put it on my bill!

CUSTOMER: Do you have spaghetti on the menu today?

WAITER: *No, I cleaned it off.*

CUSTOMER: Waiter, will
my pizza be long?

WAITER: *No sir, it will be round!*

**What did one plate say
to the other plate?**
'Dinner's on me tonight!'

Why are chefs cruel?
*Because they batter fish, beat eggs,
and whip cream*

Why did the tomato turn red?
It saw the salad dressing

**What type of cheese
is made backwards?**
Edam

What cheese do you use to hide a small horse?
Mascarpone

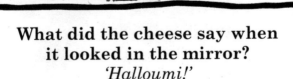

What did the cheese say when it looked in the mirror?
'Halloumi!'

What did the grape do when it got stepped on?
It let out a little wine

CUSTOMER: Waiter, how long have you worked here?

WAITER: *Six months, sir.*

CUSTOMER: Well, it can't have been you who took my order then.

CUSTOMER: Waiter, this lobster's only got one claw.

WAITER: *It must have been in a fight, sir.*

CUSTOMER: Then bring me the winner instead!

CUSTOMER: Waiter, why is my apple pie all mashed up?

WAITER: *You did ask me to 'step on it', sir!*

At some of the restaurants on holiday you can eat dirt cheap – but who wants to eat dirt?

What did the waiter say when he saw the diner put his finger in his soup?
'It's all right, it isn't hot!'

CUSTOMER: Waiter, have you got frog's legs?

WAITER: *No, sir, I always walk like this.*

CUSTOMER: Waiter, there's a dead beetle in my soup.

WAITER: *Yes, madam. Beetles are terrible swimmers.*

CUSTOMER: Waiter, this coffee tastes like mud!

WAITER: *What do you expect, sir, it was ground only a few minutes ago!*

An angry customer in a restaurant complained to the waiter that his fish was bad. The waiter picked it up, smacked it and said, 'Naughty, naughty, naughty!'

Wacky Weather

Why is England the wettest country?
Because the Queen has reigned there for years

61

It was so hot when we went on holiday that we had to take turns sitting in each other's shadow.

'I can't believe it,' said the tourist. 'I've been here an entire week and it's done nothing but rain. When do you have summer here?'

'Well, that's hard to say,' replied the local. 'Last year, it was on a Wednesday.'

Apparently last year it only rained twice. Once for six weeks and once for three months!

**What holds the sun
up in the sky?**
Sunbeams

**What goes up when the rain
comes down?**
An umbrella

**Why doesn't the sun
go to university?**
Because it has a million degrees

**What do sheep do
on sunny days?**
Have a baa-baa-cue

What bow can't be tied?
A rainbow

What does Frosty the Snowman eat for breakfast?
Snow Flakes

What goes up and down but doesn't move?
The temperature

How did you find the weather on holiday?
It was easy. I just went outside – and there it was.

What's the difference between a person with toothache and a rainstorm?
One roars with pain, the other pours with rain

**What's the weather
like out there?**
I don't know, it's too foggy to tell

**What did the tornado say
to the sports car?**
'Want to go for a spin?'

**What kind of pants
do clouds wear?**
Thunderwear

**What's a tornado's
favourite game?**
Twister

How do hurricanes see?
With one eye

**What falls but never
hits the ground?**
The temperature

**Who does everyone listen to,
but no one believes?**
The weatherman

**What is the opposite
of a cold front?**
A warm back

**What did the lightning
bolt say to the other
lightning bolt?**
'You're shocking!'

**What did the
thermometer say to
the other thermometer?**
'You make my temperature rise!'

**What's the difference between
a horse and the weather?**
*One is reined up and the other
rains down*

What did one raindrop say to the other raindrop?
'My plop is bigger than your plop.'

What do you call it when it rains chickens and ducks?
Fowl weather

What did the hurricane say to the other hurricane?
'I have my eye on you!'

What's the difference between weather and climate?
You can't weather a tree, but you can climate

What happens when it rains cats and dogs?
You have to be careful not to step in a poodle

Why did the woman go outdoors with her purse open?
Because she expected some change in the weather

How do you find out the weather when you're on holiday?
Go outside and look up

Round the World

What is the fastest country in the world?
Russia

**What is the coldest country
in the world?**
Chile

**What is a pirate's
favourite country?**
Arrrrrrgentina

**What is the slipperiest
country in the world?**
Greece

**Where did the pencil
go on holiday?**
Pennsylvania

**Why was the Egyptian
girl worried?**
Because her daddy was a mummy

Knock, knock
Who's there?
Francis
Francis who?
Francis a country in Europe

**What's the smelliest
city in America?**
Phew York

**What's the cheapest way
to get to Iceland?**
Be born there

**Where can you dance in
California?**
San Fran-disco

**What kind of cans are
there in Mexico?**
Mexicans

**How can an Irish potato
change its nationality?**
By becoming a French fry

**What has four eyes and
runs on water?**
The Mississippi

GIRL: Where does your mum come from?

BOY: *Alaska.*

GIRL: No, it's all right. I'll ask her myself.

TEACHER: Where is the English Channel?

PUPIL: *I don't know, my TV doesn't pick it up!*

Who ruled France until he exploded?
Napoleon Blownaparte

What's the funniest state in America?
Jokelahoma

In what Chinese city do they make do they make car horns?
Hong King

England doesn't have a kidney bank, but it does have a Liverpool.

I would like to go to Holland one day, wooden shoe?

I hope to go before I pop my clogs.

**In a Scandinavian race,
the last Lapp crosses
the Finnish line.**

**What do you call a boomerang
that doesn't come back?**
A stick

BOY: Will you get me a souvenir
when you go on holiday to
Australia?

GIRL: *Sure, why?*

BOY: Things made in Australia
are high koala-ty.

**Occasionally in the
Caribbean there's a total
calypso the sun.**

**Where's the best place
to buy new ties?**
Thailand

**Never make fun of a
Scotsman's traditional garb.
You could get kilt that way.**

**What do you get if you
cross a Scottish legend
with a rotten egg?**
The Loch Ness Pongster

Seeing the Sights

What rock group has four
men that don't sing?
Mount Rushmore

TEACHER: What do you know about Lake Eerie?

PUPIL: *It's full of ghosts, Miss.*

**What makes the Tower
of Pisa lean?**
It doesn't eat much

**Which cake lives in
a French cathedral?**
The Flapjack of Notre Dame

**Which kings and queens
are not buried in
Westminster Abbey?**
The ones that aren't dead yet

**What is the famous skunk
statue in Egypt?**
The Stinx

Do hamsters go on safaris?
Not safaris I know

TEACHER: What can you tell me about the Dead Sea?

PUPIL: *I didn't even know it was sick!*

What animal can jump higher than the Sydney Harbour Bridge?
All animals, because bridges can't jump

On Safari

Why are elephants wrinkled?
Have you ever tried to iron one?

**What kind of a key
opens a banana?**
A monkey

Where do chimps get their gossip?
On the ape vine

What do you get if you cross a kangaroo with a sheep?
A woolly jumper

Why do giraffes have long necks?
Because their feet smell

What is a reptile's favourite dance?
Snake, rattle and roll

**What animal
shouldn't get wet?**
A rhinoce-rust

**What's a crocodile's
favourite game?**
Snap

**What's small, furry
and bright purple?**
A koala holding its breath

**What do crocodiles
call children?**
Appetisers

**What's a koala's
favourite drink?**
Coca Koala

**Why do kangaroo mums
hate bad weather?**
Their joeys have to play inside

**What steps should you take if
you see a dangerous animal
on your travels?**
Very large ones

What do you get if you cross a sheep with a holiday resort?
The Baaahaaamaaas

A tourist was being led through the swamps of Florida.

'Is it true,' he asked, 'that an alligator won't attack you if you carry a torch?'

'That depends,' replied the guide, 'on how fast you carry the torch.'

FRIGHTENED TOURIST:
Are there any vampire bats in this cave?

GUIDE: *There were, but don't worry, the snakes ate all of them*

**What hobby does a
shark like best?**
*Anything he can sink
his teeth into*

**Why wasn't the giraffe
invited to the party?**
He was a pain in the neck

**What do you call an
elephant in a phone booth?**
Stuck

**What do you call a camel
with no humps?**
Humphrey

Why did the lion lose the card game?
Because he was playing with a cheetah

What do you call two hippos riding a bicycle?
Optimistic

What is a gorilla's favourite cookie?
Chocolate chimp

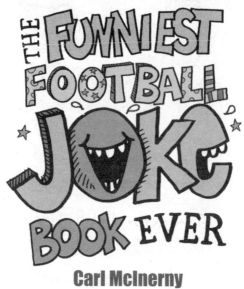

THE FUNNIEST FOOTBALL JOKE BOOK EVER

Carl McInerny

What's claret and blue and delicious? **A West Ham sandwich**

What did the ref say to the chicken who tripped a defender? **Fowl**

Why was the footballer upset on his birthday? **He got a red card**

These and many more howlers will make you laugh even if your team is losing!

9781849391115

THE FUNNIEST SPOOKY JOKE BOOK EVER

JOE KING

What happens if you see twin witches? **You won't be able to tell which witch is witch**

What did the skeleton say when his brother told a lie? **You can't fool me, I can see right through you**

What's a ghost's favourite party game? **Hide-and-shriek**

These and many more howlers will make you laugh your head off (in most cases not literally).

9781849393010

THE FUNNIEST BACK TO SCHOOL JOKE BOOK EVER

JOE KING

Why did the school bully kick the classroom computer? **Someone told him he was supposed to boot up the system**

Why did the boy come first in the 100–metre sprint? **He had athlete's foot**

Dinner lady: Eat up your greens, they are good for your skin!
Pupil: But I don't want green skin!

These and many more hilarious jokes will keep everyone chortling at playtime!

9781849395779